ISBN-10: 1-4792-3187-8

Title by Anita Eliason

The Drowning of a Seaside City
Bridgeport's Ride to Bankruptcy
Written by Sarah R. Burns
Brookfield, CT 06804
April 1994 - Published 2012

Endorsements for
THE DROWNING OF A SEASIDE CITY

"I was born in Bridgeport, I was raised in Bridgeport, and I loved Bridgeport! Thank you Ms. Burns for telling the sad story that connects the dots and makes sense of the destruction that we all witnessed."
 - Anita E, Easthampton MA

"I enjoyed the book and as an unaware Bridgeport resident am very glad for this information. It makes things clearer."
 - Carol D, Bridgeport CT

"That was a very interesting read. I was on the edge of my seat and needed some potato chips and tea to relax."
 - Deb S, Milford CT

"I found it so EXITING, INVIGERATING, FAST-PACED. Couldn't put it down."
 - Linda Y, Monroe CT

"Amazing! Thank you, Sarah. Too bad we had to wait 20 years for the real story!"
 - Mayor Mary Moran, Trumbull CT

Other books by Sarah

My Chapter Book - Jake's Adventures

http://www.amazon.com/My-Chapter-Book-Jakes-Adventures/dp/1420850598

Spiritual Healing 101

http://www.amazon.com/Spiritual-Healing-101-ebook/dp/B005XN8KH4

Contents

Foreword

This book is of interest to all who live, or have lived, in an American urban city, and who don't understand how and why the financial breakdown of these cities occurred.

Sarah Burns was part of my inner circle and witnessed first-hand, the problems Bridgeport faced in solving its financial woes. As a member of my staff as Director of the IT Department, she was highly effective in automating many city departments. She investigated and installed computer systems in over ten major departments, and was therefore, very informed of Bridgeport's operations and finances. As a Bridgeport native and long-time resident, she was well aware of Bridgeport politics.

Burns explains how the many leaders feared negative fallout at the mention of bankruptcy, and therefore took other approaches in camouflaging the city's financial issues.

Burns lived the entire bankruptcy process with me and explains in this book how Bridgeport got to that point. Bridgeport could have been the blueprint for the cities that now look for financial protection and reorganization under Chapter 9's Municipal Bankruptcy.

> Mary Chapar Moran
> Mayor 1990-1992
> City of Bridgeport, Connecticut

Dedication

This book is dedicated to all of us that have fallen in love with Bridgeport. It is dedicated to those who remember "back in the day" and what a great city it was: Thursday nights downtown, the arcade, Pleasure Beach amusement park (and that scary bridge!), Pleasure Beach ballroom record hops, the Armory record hops, Seaside Park, the bathhouse, Conte's, Ninety-Acres Park, west side roller-skating rink, huge parades, PT Barnum Midway, Beardsley Zoo, Beardsley Park, and the huge employers such as GE, Remington Arms, Remington Shaver, Bodine Manufacturing, Bridgeport Machines, and the beautiful stores - Read's, Howland's, Ray Pacific, naming only a few.

It is also dedicated to those of us born and raised there, who worked there, were just passing through, as well as local neighbors and distant lovers. It is also for those of us that are sad for its troubles and cheer for its survival and success. What a beautiful, bustling city it was, and may it quickly return to its well-deserved glory...

Acknowledgements

Most know, first-hand, about that which I write, some now know, and all were extremely helpful. They are acquaintances, colleagues, co-workers, family and friends: Steven Auerbach, Kathleen Burke, Luca Cardozo, David DeFelice, George Estrada, Mary Moran, Jocelyn Poisson, Jane Romano, Gloria Steele, Michael Daley, George Dunbar, Karla Hudacek, John Lee, Nancy Bragulat, Ruthi Hopco, Pat (Cis) Moreo, Anita Eliason, Carol DelToro, Debbie Shea, Linda Yannotti, Melinda Wilkins, Tara Alemany and Mark Gerber. Thank you for your input and support.

The Drowning of a Seaside City

Bridgeport's Ride to Bankruptcy

By Sarah R. Burns

Prologue

August 2012

I heard on the news the other day that Stockton, California was filing for bankruptcy. I decided, after much coaxing from many friends, to publish this book, which started as a thesis for a college course 18 years ago.

Bridgeport was a magical place. Just ask so many of us who were born and raised there, who still consider it "home", and care about what's going on there - even though we've moved away. The people were a beautiful, hard-working bunch, as were all those booming, behemoth factories. With a bustling downtown, Pleasure Beach, Beardsley Zoo, the yacht clubs, beautiful Seaside Park and St. Mary's by the Sea made it "the place to be." Who could ever forget Bridgeport! Our home - our love.

Bridgeport politicians let the once-manufacturing metropolis plummet without giving the shore, harbor and its location, the respect it deserved in marketing this incredible city as a destination. After 40 years, the politicians are <u>still</u> trying to develop the waterfront! Can you even believe that!? Funny how the more things change, the more they stay the same. It is 20 years later and Bridgeport is plagued by the same economic issues, as are many other American cities.

In 1990 Mayors Tom Bucci and Mary Moran were looking to relieve Bridgeport from strangling union contracts, payroll, benefits and pension burdens, and a declining tax role - and few were paying attention. Bridgeport's difference from other cities and towns was that it had continually raised taxes to balance the overgrown budget and now, this beautiful city is not desirable to many looking to relocate.

Although some benefits were gleaned from Bridgeport's bankruptcy filing due to the attention and level of awareness, those benefits have not solved the long-term problem. Chapter 9 seems to be chic these past few years - I notice that many municipalities have found restructuring protection like Stockton, California.

I have published this book to enlighten those who find it incomprehensible how municipalities get into such trouble. Being in the corporate world for many years, I, myself, found it difficult to understand. But after working for Mayor Moran for two years (1990-1992) - I learned more than I wanted to know.

Things are not always what they seem. There are crippling issues and circumstances that are never addressed, organized or publicized, which makes political moves even more difficult to understand. I hope this book provides some enlightenment.

May all our burdens be fix-able, and God Bless America's marvelous cities...

Some History

This first-hand interpretation documents what led Bridgeport to the explosive, controversial, bankruptcy filing, which awoke the nation to the plight of America's decaying cities; and how this beautiful, popular, well-loved, once-thriving city drowned in a sea of debt.

Unless you've been living under a rock, you know that America's cities are decaying rapidly. There has been very little assistance available or even offered from the state or federal government - until, of course, Mayor Mary Chapar Moran marched into the Second Circuit U.S. Court of Appeals on June 7, 1991, filing Chapter 9 for municipal restructuring under the United States Bankruptcy Code.

Did the 1991 Chapter 9 bankruptcy filing ever help Bridgeport? Did Mayor Moran have choices? If so, why did she file Bridgeport for bankruptcy?

Mayor Moran did have choices. Available options were: renegotiating burdensome union contracts, requesting a relaxation of state mandates (such as balanced budget requirements, recycling, school breakfast programs), requesting assistance from the state or federal government, raising taxes, or filing an appeal for municipal restructuring (also referred to as Municipal Bankruptcy or Chapter 9).

After many failed attempts at renegotiating the union contracts and requesting a relaxation of state mandates (and a slight tax increase), Moran chose what she believed to be Bridgeport's only option left - bankruptcy. She had two major concerns in filing Chapter 9: the city's bond rating and the reputation of the city, both of which were already in jeopardy. So in an attempt to relieve the city of escalating union contracts and benefits, outdated business tax incentives, mandated government programs and to rescue taxpayers from more outrageous tax increases, Moran filed for Chapter 9.

Bridgeport is a city of approximately 20 square miles in Fairfield County, Connecticut, approximately 60 miles northeast of New York City. The state's most populous city (153,000 in 1990), it is a port of entry at the mouth of the Pequannock River on Long Island Sound. Bridgeport was settled in 1639. Historians report that Bridgeport was originally known as Newfield and then Stratfield, and named for the first drawbridge over the river. It was taken from Stratford and Fairfield and incorporated as a city in 1836 and named Bridgeport. PT Barnum was once its mayor.

Its close proximity to all types of transportation, air, rail and sea and its accessible deep harbor were instrumental in Bridgeport's shift from agrarian to the mercantile and manufacturing industry. From the early 1900's, Bridgeport grew to be a well-known industrial center, and the city thrived producing electrical apparatus and appliances, machine tools and accessories, plastics, wiring devices and aluminum and zinc casting.

Eloquently summarized in Michael Daly's June 9, 1991 <u>Bridgeport Post</u> article, Bridgeport is described: "Industria Crescimus" is the motto of the city of Bridgeport - Latin for "By Industry We Thrive". And Bridgeport did thrive, particularly during wartime. But gone are the jobs, along with a reasonable $70 million operating budget, which made way for urban decay and $300 million operating budgets, which continue to burden the residential taxpayers.

But, City Hall continued to spend, there were always tax anticipation notes to sell, or school construction money to borrow. And when school construction bills needed to be paid, there was always another fund, or maybe next year's money to borrow. The "house" continued to grow: salaries, health benefits, pensions, tax increases in off-election years, and zero tax increases in election years.

The city's fiscal crisis was not new news and definitely no secret.

The Drowning of a Seaside City

Trail of Neglect

The trail of neglect dates back to the 1930's when Socialist Mayor Jasper McLevy was elected and served 12 consecutive terms from 1933 to 1957. McLevy resisted necessary urban renewal and modernization that other cities were undertaking, preserving his reputation and favor with taxpayers. Antiquated from neglect, Bridgeport had to be rebuilt by McLevy's successors at a higher price.

Facing re-election every two years, Bridgeport mayors have had to serve with one eye on the affairs of the city and the other on the mood of the employee unions, as well as electorate and political clubhouses that controlled their destinies. The 1991 Charter Revision, if passed, was to extend the mayoralty to a four-year term, but Bridgeport residents rejected it, reserving the option to re-elect an incumbent every two years.

In 1969, the Bridgeport legislative delegation, which included Democrat Raymond C. Lyddy and the late James McLoughlin (sons of a retired superintendent and a retired fire fighter) escorted Special Act 295 through the Connecticut Legislature. This bill created what is now referred to as the "Escalator Clause", establishing that retired police and fire officers would get the same pay raise negotiated by their active counterparts.

Four years later, Republican Mayor Nicholas A. Panuzio began his tenure with a 1973 approved budget of $72 million and an estimated budget balance (also known as surplus) of $600,000. A change in accounting methods, at that time, allowed the city to include anticipated revenue in its budget (although not yet received), resulting in a skyrocketed budget balance from $600,000 to $3.8 million. This was an election year and the implementation of the "fire and police 20 year retirement giveaway", in which fire and police retired with full pension after 20 years of service.

Democrat John C. Mandanici took office for two terms, from 1978 through 1981 beginning with a $100 million approved budget, a $7.0 million budget balance and ending with a $128 million approved budget and an $8.8 million balance. Mandanici is credited with the teachers' binding arbitration law (binding arbitration is a process by which a mediator settles disputes when labor and management are unable to settle their differences). He took a fast stand with striking Bridgeport school teachers - and about 200 teachers landed in jail. He also chose to fight, rather than settle, a number of federal discrimination suits regarding Fire Department examinations costing the city millions of dollars in court awards.

In 1982 Republican Leonard Paoletta captured the mayoralty until 1986. Finances began to slide. Paoletta started with a $128 million approved budget and a $6.2 million deficit and ended 1985 with a

$171 million approved budget and a $5.6 million deficit.

The electorate voted-in Democrat Thomas Bucci in November 1986, and in January 1987 he began his tenure with the $5.6 million deficit that Paoletta had projected and the fireworks began.

In Millions

Term	Mayor	Beginning Budget	Expected Balance	Ending Budget	Actual Balance
1971-1975	Nicholas Panuzio	72.0	0.6	100.0	3.8
1976-1981	John Mandanici	100.0	7.0	128.0	8.8
1982-1984	Leonard Paoletta	128.0	(6.2)	171.0	(5.6)
1985-1989	Thomas Bucci	171.0	(5.6)	278.0	(51.0)
1990-1992	Mary Moran	278.0	(16.0)	320.0	(20.0)
1993-2003	Joe Ganim	320.0	-	-	-
2004-2007	John Fabrizi	428.4	(7.2)	-	-
2008-curr	Bill Finch	517.8	-	-	-

Some of these numbers were difficult to find.
I'm sure you get the idea by now.

Whew - confusing huh? Even for you finance veterans! Wondering why these numbers don't match? Yeah, me too and I researched all the budget documents! Mandanici ending with an $8.8 million balance and Paoletta beginning his tenure with a $5.6 million deficit? It has something to do with expected balance vs. actual balance (or gap - some accrual vs. actual accounting method or a combination thereof?), and throw in a little "accounting duplicity." Some budgets considered revenue before it was received, and then, maybe - did not receive it at all or commonly overestimated revenue projections. And some numbers on the expenditure side, did not consider already negotiated union raises, that must be given that year by law through collective bargaining and binding arbitration agreements.

Variable expenses could be staggering to a municipality. City pensions were unfunded, meaning that pension money must be budgeted each year because it had not been anticipated, accumulated and invested. Ergo, early unexpected retirements, along with snow plowing, new union contracts, binding arbitration agreements, government mandates like recycling, and law suits could drastically throw-off a balanced budget.

For example, the <u>Connecticut Post</u> reported that in December 1993, the U.S. District Court in Bridgeport awarded a $2 million settlement to the owner of an aircraft sales company concluding that "Bridgeport had tried to depress the value of Scap's property so that it could later acquire it at a cheaper price." This money comes from the operating budget.

Disclosure - Awareness & Fireworks

In February of 1988 Mayor Bucci disclosed a $51 million budget gap! The Bridgeport Regional Business Council (BRBC - which is like a Chamber of Commerce for the Bridgeport area) formed a steering committee, and the State of Connecticut authorized Bridgeport to sell $60 million in municipal bonds. Municipal bonds are monies advanced to the city from the sale of bonds which are something like a company's stock and to be used for capital purchases only. The purpose was to retire debt and provide working capital for the city. The state established the Bridgeport Financial Review Board (also known as the Financial Review Board, BFRB and FRB - I'll use Financial Review Board and FRB as clarity dictates) to oversee the city's financials and operations. The FRB hired Ukeles Associates Inc. to analyze and overhaul municipal procedures. Accounting methods reverted back to including revenue on hand only (not anticipated revenue) by order of the State Legislature. By July of 1988 the Financial Review Board met for the first time and began imposing financial discipline on the city.

August 1988 witnessed the formation of the Bridgeport Regional Business Council's Management Advisory Committee (MAC). MAC was to carry out the Ukeles recommendations and reform City Hall. Ten task forces and 17 loaned executives from local businesses were activated to address the Police, Fire, Development and Public Works Departments.

The following excerpt from Dr. George Dunbar's book <u>Back From Broke</u> clearly reveals Bridgeport's state of affairs:

> Richard P. Bodine, owner and president of one of Bridgeport's oldest manufacturing firms, Bodine Manufacturing, was the first chairman of MAC. In a letter to Bucci in July, 1989, Bodine wrote:

> The fiscal crisis in Bridgeport is very real, and the future of the city is very much at risk. A successful recovery cannot be guaranteed without full cooperation of labor, management, the private sector, political interests and neighborhood community groups. Political leadership and the taxpayers of the city must become persuaded that money will have to be spent up front to realize major savings in the future. This is a concept widely known and accepted in the private sector but very difficult to get accepted in the public sector.

> The constraints that have been identified as detrimental to the adoption of modern management practices - i.e., an obsolete charter, and certain restrictive clauses in

14

collective bargaining agreements can no longer be accepted as "the way things are". This is a luxury the city can no longer afford. The courage and enormous effort required to effect change must be brought to bear. The management and organizational changes recommended in this report can, if vigorously implemented, lead Bridgeport to recovery.

The Task Force recommendations began implementation in July of 1989. In November 1989 the voters "shoot the messenger." They "throw-out" Bucci and elect Mary Chapar Moran, the first woman mayor whose promise was to professionalize City Hall.

The Drowning of a Seaside City

Mary Moran is Elected!

Between February and May of 1990, a new professional consideration policy was adopted in filling new administrative jobs. The reporting structure was revised from an overwhelming 34 departments reporting directly to the mayor, to seven; and all service departments reported to the newly appointed Chief Administrative Officer (CAO) George R. Dunbar.

The Charter Revision Commission was formed in May 1990 and by December 1990 the Five Year Restructuring Plan began with the formation of city employee and community representative teams. The Financial Review Board and other community groups approved the Five Year Restructuring Plan in January of 1991 which outlined 52 projects with a $68 million savings over a five year period. Implementation began in March 1991, but this was not to solve the current year's financial problems.

Tony Hernandez, Certified Public Accountant and owner of a successful CPA firm in Bridgeport, was well-regarded, knowledgeable, considered a city activist, and always concerned about the people of Bridgeport and its financials. Hernandez approached the mayor on the topic of bankruptcy while she was running for mayor and again after she was elected. Hernandez had previously claimed the city would realize a $20 million budget gap. But no one took him seriously. "He told me I'd be surprised at the mess that I was going to find. It's not that I didn't believe him. But... I felt by bringing in the professionals, by starting to streamline government, by making people more accountable, by watching the spending - all those things that work in industry - that we would be able to see the light at the end of the tunnel" Moran said. However, Moran quickly realized that a municipality cannot be run like a business. Private business focuses on profits, making decisions that will positively affect the bottom-line. A municipality must consider social needs, union constraints and public perception in decision making, which oftentimes negatively impacts the bottom-line. Yes, both should be considered - but typically, the bottom-line suffers.

Hernandez sent Moran a report on the city's insolvency and indicated there was no alternative but bankruptcy. Tax collections were slowing, the regional economy declining, welfare costs soaring, and the city's Grand List (list of taxable properties) sliding. As Moran focused on the Five-Year Restructuring Plan and other efforts to improve City Hall, she realized that there would be a projected accumulated deficit of over $250,000 million in five years. More than a quarter billion dollars!

Solving the Problems

People had solutions - or thought they did. The three most popular suggestions for fixing the city's budget were:

1. Reduce, if not eliminate Welfare.
2. Return or sell Mayor Moran's new car.
3. Layoff more city workers.

Some thought city assets should be sold. These suggestions sound feasible in theory, but won't work in the real world.

1. To eliminate Welfare was out of the question. The sociological ramifications would be staggering, not to mention the legal entanglements. Although most people believe that welfare recipients are lazy and do not want to work, that is far from the truth. Most welfare clients are single mothers, senior citizens and factory workers who are not easily re-trainable for new-tech jobs. Welfare, also known as Income Maintenance or Aid to the Poor, is a state mandated and state funded program supported by the federal government. Eliminating welfare is not just a "city-thing" which can be easily removed. Bridgeport's 1990-1991 annual budget for Welfare was over $17 million; and although 90% of the city's welfare expense is

reimbursed from the state, the city still pays the cost of maintaining the program salaries, office equipment, system upgrades and the like.

Most indigent locate in the city for that is where they get their welfare checks, food stamps and any health care they may require. The suburbs, surrounding towns of Fairfield, Stratford, and Trumbull, do not have hospitals, low income housing or shelters, nor do they administer any income maintenance. Bridgeport carries the financial, social and infrastructure burden of the region's needy.

2. Ahh - the new car. The truth is, this car was budgeted and ordered (before Moran was in office) from the bond money Bucci secured (remember this money is for capital purchases only). The old car was becoming costly to repair and the new car was actually cheaper to operate (the car did not come out of any operating budget, whereas all repairs do).

Another fact most voters never learned from the news media, was that Moran reassigned back to the police force, the $48,000 a year police officer who was assigned to drive her. She mostly drove herself where she needed to go, requiring a reliable, efficient car. Her predecessors all had a $48,000 a year driver (remember this was 1990!! That salary would equate to around $85,000 now!). So even if she had bought the car with operating money, she still would have saved the difference between the car, the repairs and the driver's salary!

3. The number of full time city employees had already been cut from 4,473 in 1986 to 3,378 in 1990 (a reduction of 25% in four years). Safety and services were already being compromised and Moran felt any more reductions would seriously affect the well being of Bridgeport's residents.

All options were being considered. The selling of the city's assets, while a good idea for immediate cash, would be a temporary solution only. The escalating costs of future budgets would not be resolved by selling revenue generating assets such as Beardsley Park, Fairchild Wheeler Golf Course or the Bridgeport Sikorsky Airport (located in Stratford).

Being disgusted with high taxes, low service and high crime, some taxpayers demanded Mayor Moran start bankruptcy proceedings. Bridgeport taxpayers pay about double in property tax as, for example, Fairfield residents. In 1990, a house assessed at $100,000 in Fairfield would pay about $3,000 taxes while a Bridgeport home owner would pay about $6,000 on a $100,000 assessment. Bridgeport taxpayers were, and still are, very angry. Many believed that the high taxes were not in line with values, services and most of all, perception of safety.

Members of the Bridgeport Taxpayers Association's Executive Board met on February 20, 1991 with Mayor Moran, her Chief Financial Officer Richard Robinson, Policy and Management Director Mahesh Reddy and Mayoral Aide David DeFelice to announce their intention to force the bankruptcy filing. Moran explained the possible long-term effects a bankruptcy petition could have on the city, such as adversely affect bond and credit ratings as well as economic development possibilities. She also expressed her frustration and urged the group to contact and ask their legislators to work with her administration in overturning onerous mandates, like state welfare and binding arbitration. When asked, Moran admitted that taxes would most likely have to be increased.

Moran's staff was making huge strides in streamlining departments and implementing efficient, effective procedures while being fiscally responsible. The Management Information and Communication Systems (MICS - known today as Information Technology or IT) Department accomplished major improvement projects using $493,000 of bond money. The following 10 departments were among many that were computerized and upgraded with appropriate systems, providing accuracy, efficiency and a 12 month return on investment: Computer Room, Police Call And Dispatch (CAD aka 911), Engineering, Fire Training, Personnel, Golf Course, Print Shop, Public Works, Beardsley Zoo and Welfare.

A total of $72,000 in annual cost savings was also realized by restructuring the phone system: restricting telephone long distance calls, removing unused or inactive telephone lines, implementing a 411 information block, and inventory of and reduction to the maximum number of lines allowed under the current in-force SNET three-year billing contract. This was accomplished by one department within 18 months.

The Drowning of a Seaside City

No Good Solutions

But, there were some major expense issues that were not repairable by the city's administration. State mandated education spending (state law dictates the dollar amount of all municipal education budgets), Police and Fire retirement contracts (remember that "Escalator Clause" from 1969?), Civil Service and Supervisors Union contracts (typically a 6% raise in salary each year), health, vacation and sick pay benefits (city employees accumulate 2.5 vacation and sick days per month (1.25 each) and some unions having unlimited sick leave) were some of the main issues in deciding the Chapter 9 filing. Additional factors such as the burden of providing social services (Welfare, hospitals, courts, Motor Vehicle, low income housing) for the region's needy without help from the suburbs, and declining assistance from the federal and state government were contributing issues.

Moran struggled with an anticipated $16 million budget gap on an approved 1990-91 budget of $278 million (down from $285 in 1989-1990). Despite months of negotiations with the city's 13 unions, concession talks had failed and compromises on automatic salary increases or furloughs were not likely. Some departmental budgets were cut as much as 25%, and city services were being seriously impacted.

Some fire and police unions had already negotiated some slight wage give-backs, but city union officials refused to negotiate any further wage or benefit adjustments. And after testifying in Washington regarding America's cities in financial crisis, Moran contacted President George Bush for help and consideration. There was no response and no assistance.

Bankruptcy Filing - Not So Easy!

On June 7th 1991, the city declares bankruptcy!

"This action should assure long-term stability and fiscal restructuring that will afford much-needed tax relief and provide the services our residents deserve," Mayor Moran said in a prepared statement to Bridgeport's Common Council.

There would be two parts to this Chapter 9 filing for Bridgeport:

1. ***To establish "Home Rule".*** Upon the bankruptcy rumblings, just after Moran was elected, the state presented a Distressed Cities Legislation (Home Rule). Had this passed the regular session of the Connecticut General Assembly, it would have precluded Bridgeport's ability to file for bankruptcy without the governor's blessing. Moran explained that as being the reason for excluding the Common Council from her decision to declare insolvency until after the fact. She exercised the city's autonomy and filed Chapter 9 before the state passed the bill, which would have relinquished the city's 'Home Rule' (authority to file bankruptcy without the states permission).

2. ***To prove insolvency.*** The $16 million budget
gap by the end of the fiscal year (August
1991) was the insolvency part. Although the
city still had some money in the bank, the city
would be out of money by August if it did not
raise taxes. Many did not realize that a police
overtime project would have "eaten that
money up" in no time. There is no budgeting
the money required to satisfy an unexpected
emergency, (such as "9-11" for New York
City). I've seen as much as $2 million
budgeted for Police and Fire overtime.
Moran walked into court with good intentions
still having "a few bucks in the bank." Now
wait and see how confusing that gets.

Moran charged Governor Weicker with turning a
deaf ear to her urgent pleas for help. He simply told
her to raise taxes, exclaiming he had troubles of his
own - he didn't even have a state budget! Moran also
charged that the Financial Review Board stuck to its
narrow role, which did not include setting policy. It
refused to participate in union concession talks and
lobby for legislative changes in binding arbitration,
heart and hypertension benefits and restore property
tax relief that would have saved millions.

Moran left no stone unturned including a request to
the Connecticut Resources Recovery Authority
(CRRA - the garbage to energy plant) about
renegotiating its contractual annual $1.7 million
payment in lieu of $11 million in taxes. The CRRA
would not negotiate unless Moran approved their

expansion plan. Due to environmental issues and area resident concerns, Moran did not support an expansion. Soooo - no help there! I was surprised to find that a few members of the Financial Review Board also sat on the CRRA Board.

Mahesh Reddy, Moran's Director of Office of Policy and Management (OPM - in charge of the coordination and preparation of the city's budget, budget process, and who also assisted in preparing the city's bankruptcy petition), believed that it was easy for critics to oppose all ideas, but no one was offering alternatives to a high tax increase or bankruptcy. Reddy could not be convinced, that raising taxes would solve the city's future fiscal problems, not even for the next five years.

Alice Lipowicz's <u>Bridgeport Post</u> article revealed sympathy for Bridgeport's financial crisis but lawmakers agreed that federal relief was unlikely:

> I do not see the federal government stepping in to come to the financial rescue of all the cities facing financial problems. I think the federal government has got to be more involved for the long term in helping to improve the economic base of the cities, Rep. Christopher Shays, R-4, said in an interview.
>
> One of the problems is that in 1980 federal dollars made up about 17 percent of local budgets. Now the federal government provides only six percent of the budgets of

our local communities. We're now beginning to see the effects of those policy decisions, Senator Christopher Dodd D-Conn said.

Manufacturing jobs have been lost, municipal incomes are declining, and more communities may face the same kind of crisis Bridgeport is experiencing if the nation's economy is not turned around soon, said Senator Joseph I. Liebermann D-Conn.

We're not miracle workers, Dodd said. There isn't a pool of funds out there that says 'bankrupt cities'.

One of the larger controversies involved the union pensions. Unfunded pension liabilities, as listed in the bankruptcy petition, totaled $346 million, which represented the amount due all retired employees and active workers who had qualified for pensions. Union leaders believed that the union pensions were secure, stating that pension contributions are a primary obligation of the city, and that obligation would not be relieved because of the bankruptcy filing. However, attorney Richard Zeisler told reporters that all executory contracts, or agreements which are to be performed in the future, would be renegotiated if they were "onerous and economically burdensome."

Zeisler's opinion was shared by two leading experts on municipal bankruptcy, James E. Spiotto of Chapman & Cutler of Chicago and Dale R.

Brockmeier of Harding & Ogborn of Denver. They told the <u>Bridgeport Post</u> that a municipality can avoid its executory contracts if the court accepts the petition.

The Drowning of a Seaside City

The Challenges Continue

And union leaders were angry:

> "She [Moran] has met with us for the past two months. This [bankruptcy filing] had to have been in her mind all the time," said Ann Twigg, president of the city's National Association of Governmental Employees units.

> "It's union busting and a political ploy..." added NAGE Business Agent Wayne Gilbert.

> "She's made the city, unions, review board and everybody else a pawn - someone to point a finger at," said Olsen, [Financial Review Board member, who is also the state president of the AFL-CIO].

Governor Weicker's position was clear. He felt that the solution was to raise taxes. If there was not the political will in Bridgeport to do that, then that's why the Financial Review Board was formed.

The FRB unanimously adopted a $320 million budget for the 1991-1992 fiscal year and directed the council to raise taxes 18 percent to 71.2 mills. That would be a property tax of $7,120 a year, $593 a month on that $100,000 home we spoke of before. The taxpayers were wild!

Most common council members did not support Moran in the bankruptcy filing but offered no alternative solutions. They also refused to impose such a tax increase. Not only was this increase totally ridiculous, it would be political suicide. They clearly would not be re-elected by the taxpayers! Donald A. Kirshbaum, the FRB Executive Director, intended to seek a court order compelling the 20 Common Council representatives to raise taxes. Treasurer Francisco L. Borges, suggested a takeover of major city departments and to state-impose a City Manager. Kirshbaum stated, "I do not believe that it is possible for the city or the FRB to balance this year's budget. The only tool available to the Board is a meat ax."

The FRB also discussed impeaching Mayor Moran. She would not follow their directives and they were furious. The City of Bridgeport operated then and continues to operate under an elected Mayor and elected City Council (also know as Common Council). Mayor Moran made it very clear that they could not impeach her. She was elected, she had no intention of resigning and would even seek re-election. Moran encouraged the council to adopt the (then present) 60.3 mill rate until the bankruptcy issue was resolved, and they did.

Attorney Dale R. Brockmeier of Denver, Colorado, considered an expert in municipal bankruptcy, said the city must satisfy four legal conditions before a federal judge would allow the petition to stand. The petitioner must be:

1. *A municipality.* Bridgeport is legally a municipality as stated in the State of Connecticut Register and Manual (a municipality being defined as "a city or town having its own incorporated government for local affairs").

2. **Willing to reorganize its debt and tax structure.** The fact that Moran filed the bankruptcy petition states the willingness to reorganize debt and tax structure.

But is the city insolvent and does it have legal authority to file Chapter 9? These last two conditions were to be the "kickers."

3. *Insolvent.* Under Chapter 9 of the United States Bankruptcy Code, a municipality must demonstrate to the court that it is insolvent - that its liabilities exceed its assets. It then allows an insolvent municipality to reorganize and adjust its debt under the leadership of a federal judge (a delay in paying debts while arranging payment schedules with creditors). Unlike Chapter 11 or 13 for businesses and individuals, Chapter 9 does not force or allow a city's assets to be sold to pay creditors, nor does it remove city official's governing powers. In 1976, Congress made Section 365 applicable to Chapter 9, providing a distressed

municipality with an opportunity to assume or reject executory contracts, including collective bargaining agreements. For municipalities burdened by labor contracts and pension plans they cannot afford, this provision may have been the most important and unique feature of Chapter 9 (remember that fire and police pension benefits escalation law passed through Connecticut's Congress?). Chapter 9 filings in recent years have been exercised by school districts, hospitals and special taxing districts. Bridgeport was, by far, the largest city to seek protection under this code.

The real confusion started when the issue of the infamous $25 million cash reserve was raised. The Financial Review Board required the city to have a $25 million revenue fund balance (cash reserve on hand) and that money could not be used for operating expenses or capital purchases. This 'intercept fund', as it was referred to, was to protect the holders of the $200 million in municipal bonds. When Moran filed the bankruptcy petition the city had the $25 million in the bank but the FRB would not let the city use that money. They declared that the city had over $46 million in the bank and was paying their bills. Frankly, I am yet to determine how the state arrived at the $46 million figure. Moran should have spent the $25 million and the other $11 million that the state said

Bridgeport had on-hand, but the FRB would not let her spend that "intercept money". SO - was the city REALLY bankrupt!?

When Chief Financial Officer, Richard Robinson was asked by Bankruptcy Judge Alan H.W. Shiff if the city had to pay back the money [the $25 million reserve] before the end of the fiscal year, where would the city get the money? Robinson replied, "I don't mean to be flip, but we'd have to rob a bank. Outside of borrowing, we could have a special levy. Otherwise, there's no way to foreseeably do that." Robinson continued "...We are not broke. We have not spent our last dollar. I foresee the day when we will."

Reddy (remember, he was Moran's OPM Director in charge of the budget) said that the city would be out of cash by September if it could not use the $25 million.

The accounting controversy continued and, when in court, the state continued to claim that the $25 million was available to the city. But, when out of court, insisted that the city could not spend that money! Huh? What?? Talk about a mixed message! The state was angry and trying to stop Moran from claiming bankruptcy. Why? Because there were other Connecticut towns and cities paying attention, waiting to do the same to relieve their overburdened budgets.

4. ***Generally authorized by the state to file for bankruptcy.*** The next and final issue was to be whether the city had the authorization to file Chapter 9. This is the other "kicker." Brockmeier stated that "...there's lots of case law out there that says if you've got the power to incur debt and contract for debt - you've got the power to reorganize debt..." meaning the city could make a case for having the power and authority to claim bankruptcy.

But, Attorney General Richard Blumenthal challenged Bridgeport's legal authority, stating that, "It's simply impermissible for any municipality to unilaterally declare bankruptcy... in legal terms, it's an act that is null and void, as far as the State of Connecticut is concerned." Brockmeier said challenging Bridgeport's authority to file was a jurisdictional issue which failed to get to the root of the city's problems, "I'm not sure it does anybody any good to object to the filing. All it does is provide a forum. All you need is one year's big tax to set off a parade of horribles... It's like dropping a neutron bomb. You'll still have plenty of houses, but there won't be any people left." Most non-political, informed people recognized the problem and the solution.

However, Blumenthal counterpoints in his <u>Commercial Law Bulletin</u> article: "..The

Tenth Amendment to the Constitution, which forbids infringement on state sovereignty specifically acknowledged... Chapter 9 does not limit the power of the state to control, by legislation or otherwise, a municipality in the exercise of its political or governmental power, including expenditures for the exercise of those powers. Before a bankruptcy court may approve a plan, the city must obtain all of the necessary approvals of state agencies affected by the plan - which means that a state may be free to block a plan if it chooses to do so."

A major concern of the city, which could also become a legal issue, according to Brockmeier, was the bond holders. A signed agreement, in the Fall of 1989, that the city was financially sound at the sale of the bonds, raised the question whether bond holders could sue the city and the underwriters for securities fraud. At the sale, the city appeared financially sound. It was not until December 1990 that Mayor Moran discovered the $16 million gap.

A major concern of the state was that the city's credit rating could take a dive. Well, it wasn't going to dive far. Even with state guarantees and backing, the city's bonds were rated below investment grade level. Moody's Investors Services said the suspension of ratings on the city's uninsured general obligation bonds occurred gave Bridgeport a BAA, or its lowest investment-grade rating in November when the city sold $19.25 million in bonds. Standard & Poor did not take any action on the city's rating.

The state was still trying to claim that Bridgeport did not have the authority to enter into a bankruptcy petition without the approval of the state. But it was already clear that Bridgeport could enter the bankruptcy claim without the states permission or approval.

Bankruptcy Denied!!!

August 2nd 1991 - Federal Bankruptcy Judge Alan H. W. Shiff declares the city is **not bankrupt!**

After all that 'hoopla,' Judge Shiff determines that Bridgeport did have the right to file bankruptcy, but that they were not bankrupt.

Barbara Hankin and Richard Zeisler explain:

> For purposes of Chapter 9, a municipality may be found to be insolvent if it is "generally not paying its debts as they become due...; or [if it is] unable to pay its debts as they become due..."

> "Bridgeport's demonstration of financial distress was not sufficient to fulfill the insolvency required to maintain a Chapter 9 petition ... it is necessary for a Chapter 9 debtor to establish the foresee ability of insolvency as of the petition date based on a cash flow rather than budget gap analysis with the foreseeable period limited to the current fiscal year or, based on an adopted budget, in its next fiscal year..."

By October of 1991 Moran filed a bankruptcy appeal; and the Charter revision was completed and approved by the Common Council.

The Drowning of a Seaside City

Moran OUT & The "Magic" Continues

In November 1991 the Charter revision (the four year mayoral term among other necessary revisions which would have helped the city operate more efficiently) and Mayor Moran are defeated in the election.

Joe Ganim is elected mayor and withdraws the bankruptcy petition after securing union compromises, furloughs and selling (revenue generating) Beardsley Park to the state and (supposedly) balances the budget without a tax increase!? Wow - who knew it was that easy?! After his first year in office the union raises were back in effect, patronage jobs were paid higher than in Moran's administration and employee furloughs were no longer mandated.

Sounds like magic - doesn't it? It is, with smoke and mirrors, still. Where did the $16 million gap go? Bridgeport tax rolls were still declining. Grand List figures in 1990 were 2.344 million; 1991 - 2,336 million; 1992 - 2,309 million, and 42% of the Grand List was non-taxable properties (schools, hospitals, churches, non-profits).

And the money had not yet been received from the sale of the zoo. But the Financial Review Board allowed Mayor Ganim to count the "zoo money" to balance the budget. This sale had been tied-up in court by Beardsley's heirs who were suing the city for the illegal sale of the Beardsley property. As of 1992, the Beardsley heirs lost their suit and the sale of the zoo to the state stands.

For the November 1992 election, the Charter Revision committee eliminated the four year mayoral term from the revisions, in order to get the other important items passed and it worked. The charter revisions were passed without the mayoral term increase to four years. (The four-year term was eventually passed, during Ganim's second tenure.)

A commercial aid program for distressed areas, designed to create jobs and development was announced by President Clinton on January 17, 1994. A distressed city could receive up to $100 million through this program if it met the poverty criteria and offered a revitalization plan.

And as city officials rushed off to Washington to apply for the $100 million aid program [Federal Grant] Ganim touts, "I think we've really got a shot."

> "One of our assets is also one of our problems," Liebermann said. "Our cities have some very serious problems. They have a high rate of joblessness and skyrocketing local taxes... This is intended to break the whole cycle."
> He and other Bridgeport officials said the troubled city's flirtation with bankruptcy three

years ago may help move it to the forefront in the application process.

"We feel strongly, and people in Washington confirm, that because [former mayor] Mary Moran attempted to file for bankruptcy, it put Bridgeport on the map as a city in need," said Bridgeport Regional Business Council Vice President Roberta Burns-Howard.

Marvin Fast, spokesman for Senator Christopher Dodd, said Connecticut cities have a good chance at being selected, "Connecticut certainly has three of the poorest cities in the country, we have a case to make - these cities are screaming for help."

All the players acknowledged the seriousness of Bridgeport's problems, but offered no reasonable do-able solutions, yet continued to criticize Moran for filing the bankruptcy petition.

If Tom Bucci hadn't declared insolvency in 1989 and Mary Moran hadn't filed bankruptcy in 1991, things might not have looked so optimistic in 1994! It's a shame the general voting public is typically ill-informed and "shoots the messenger."

Mayor Moran's Bridgeport Chapter 9 Bankruptcy filing WAS the answer!

The Drowning of a Seaside City

Epilogue
August 2012

While I prefer to not minimize anyone's value, the union raises and benefits packages at the time, were beyond competitive and more than bordered on greed. Greed always gets someone into trouble. And in this case, a lot of people were in trouble; taxpayers, mostly, who had to pay for the greed, and eventually those that benefited and lived at those means wind-up having the rug pulled out when the greed flow is stopped. I see many towns and cities are renegotiating union pensions to almost nothing. I also read that many municipal workers retire with a pension value of more than their working salary. That's due to being able to bank sick and vacation days into their pension fund. While it sounds like a nice benefit, it cannot be sustained over decades, and there goes that rug again - pulled out from under. It's better to re-negotiate those benefits, than have a city go into bankruptcy and have the power shift. But employees and unions do not, typically, like giving anything up, so bankruptcy becomes the only answer.

Bridgeport has had a total of 53 mayors. There have been three mayors since bankruptcy-toting Mayor Moran: Joe Ganim (who went to jail in 2003 for corruption); John Fabrizi (who was arrested for drug use and decided not to run again in 2007); and the current Bill Finch. I knew these fellows back then, all nice men too, but caught-up in "the game".

In July 1998, during Joe Ganim's tenure, Bridgeport's $16 million Harbor Yard was erected. Harbor Yard is a 5,300 seat baseball arena and entertainment complex. The internet reports it being funded through public and team contributions. I guess they didn't receive "the" money from Washington. If they did, I don't know where it went. My guess would have been to build Harbor Yard. I recently noticed that Harbor Yard is now being called Webster Bank Arena. I had heard that the complex was in trouble. Apparently Webster Bank has steppe-up and funded this beautiful venue. Thank you, Webster.

As of July 2012, Bridgeport touts the beginning of the long-awaited development of Harborpoint, aka Harbor Point, Steel Point and Steel Point Harbor (development of the deep harbor area previously known as Carpenter Steel) with a retail giant sports pro shop (Pro Bass) recently signing-on as its first resident. We'll see. I'll believe it when I walk into the store and buy something. Here is an interesting website that chats about this (http://www.city-data.com/forum/connecticut/588418-steel-point-harbor-bridgeport.html).

I have spent all day researching updated stats and find only a few numbers that can be compared to previous years. The 2013 mill rate is a little over 41 mills which equates to about $4,100 in taxes on a home assessed at $100,000. The 2011 population was approximately 144,000 compared to over 153, 000 in 1990. And the 2011 taxable Net Grand List is around $88 million. I finally found "one number" for the 2013 or 2012 Approved Budget - $517.8 million.

Back in 1990, the state mandate was that a property re-evaluation (referred to as re-val) must be done every 10 years and taxes adjusted accordingly. Moran had the re-val done, but refused to implement the tax implications on that re-val, which would have raised taxes because property values had gone up.

A re-val tax implication delay is good news for property owners, because taxes typically never go down. A re-evaluation will change property assessment numbers, which changes tax amounts.

In October 2008, a full property re-evaluation was done. Since then, the re-val laws have been slightly revamped, and now require a five-year interim property re-val. The interim re-val is typically a comparable property evaluation rather than a "walk-around" evaluation, which can be the good news and the bad news. Property improvements through permits are reflected in value, while property decline is not necessarily reflected in the new value.

It appears that Mayor Finch has included the cost of this interim re-val in the 2013 budget, scheduled to take place sometime in 2013. Hopefully, the 2013 interim re-val will show lower home values. Hmpf - the good news and the bad news!

Now, typically one would think if property value goes down, taxes go down. Not so fast. Don't spend that money yet. If taxes go down, city revenue goes down, and then there's a need to raise the mill-rate (taxes) to compensate for the loss in property value (assessment) which, in turn, provides income (revenue) for the city. And we know that budgets never go down! The would be a too good, too easy answer - wouldn't it? Taxes down - Budget down. Taxpayers happy. Yea. Not likely.

I'm sorry that I am not providing the typical summary that you can wrap your head around, but it's business as usual, as John Lee's article below helps my position. And I think someone should make a movie out of this story. There's about 10 of us available to help with the details; those of us who worked very closely with Moran trying to repair the damage, and fix the problems, while increasing service and perception: Sarah Burns, Mary Moran, Steven Auerbach, Kathleen Burke, Luca Cardozo, David DeFelice, George Estrada, Jocelyn Poisson, Jane Romano, and Gloria Steele.

Well, it's funny-money and balance-the-budget on the backs-of-the-taxpayers again, as quoted in this April 2012 Connecticut Post article by John Marshall Lee:

> Mayor Bill Finch wants a 7 percent tax increase, an increase of 2.7 mills and people in Bridgeport are saying "NO" loud and clear at public hearings. Since 2008 he claims that

he has cut more than 225 positions, but the evidence in the budget charts are that 178 were in education, over which he claims no accountability. Forty-eight positions over five years is not much real cutting. There is more cutting available and necessary!

Look at city personnel positions that are approved each year and go unfilled. Last year Mayor Finch proposed more than 60 of them. They cost taxpayers about $5 million annually. There should be no "ghost positions" approved by the City Council. And there are "ghost expenses" budgeted throughout departments that are never spent for the line items proposed and approved by the City Council. For example, the legislative budget, to fund the City Council, contains almost $200,000 annually of such unaccounted-for expense. Your tax dollars disappear without you, the taxpayer, knowing where because there is no June monthly revenue, expense and variance report where you could check what was spent in each line item. Mayor Finch calls this "budget transparency." It is obviously not. Nor is it accountable. Other mayors might call it "funny business." I call it an illegal avoidance of clear charter language to keep the public ignorant.

Let's look at the justification for increasing taxes:

Reform of Bridgeport's education system serving 20,300 students is primary. Reform needed with a price tag of $7 million from the city, an increase of 5 percent, to trigger a state increase of 2.5 percent. The city can afford this increase by eliminating the ghost expenses easily. The education department will set up an accountability fiscal watchdog group with internet reporting to provide real "budget transparency." We need to encourage real teeth for these watchdogs!

Pension obligations are the mayor's second reason for the 7 percent increase. In the Connecticut Post last week he said: "I've proposed ... a $10.5 million increase targeted to the closed Plan A." The mayor's budget math is once again wrong. The 2012 current budget indicates that we will spend $4.5 million before July 1, 2012, on this item. The 2013 budget indicates $10.5 million, an increase of $6 million, not $10.5 million. The mayor should make public the plan he finally negotiated with the state before the last election. Why are the terms of the agreement becoming known to us only now? Publish the agreement you bound us to, please. Funding for police and fire pensions in the coming year reduces City Pension B funding by $2.3 million, so decrease the $6 million request down to $3.7 million net.

Economic development has failed to produce net gains during the Finch administration. The 2013 budget book shows Net Grand List for 2007 and 2008. Why? Last year's budget showed the 2010 Net Grand List. Are we going backward? How competent are the people putting the city numbers and narrative together for the taxpayer and council to consider? And if we are not developing new tax base with new development, why should any non-union employees get a raise?

They say Bridgeport is turning the corner - and what corner would that be?

Such a shame for such a beautiful ***Seaside City***...

The Drowning of a Seaside City

Some Great Links

City of Bridgeport:
www.bridgeportct.gov

NY Times article:
www.nytimes.com/1991/08/02/nyregion/us-judge-blocks-bridgeport-from-bankruptcy-court.html

Only In Bpt:
www.onlyinbridgeport.com/wordpress/

John Marshall Lee:
www.onlyinbridgeport.com/wordpress/?s=John+marshall+lee

Webster Bank Arena / Harbor Yard:
www.websterbankarena.com/

Greater Bridgeport Symphony:
www.gbs.org/

Klein Memorial:
www.fairfieldtheatre.org/

East Enders:
www.east-enders.itgo.com/